Ice Cream

INSPIRATION

ISBN 13: 978-1-4621-4648-2
ebook ISBN 13: 978-1-4621-4770-0

Published by Front Table Books, an imprint of Cedar Fort, Inc.
2373 W. 700 S., Suite 100, Springville, UT 84663
Distributed by Cedar Fort, Inc., www.cedarfort.com

Library of Congress Registration Number: 2024930097

Photos by Melissa B. Howell
Cover design and interior layout and design by Shawnda T. Craig

Printed in Colombia

10 9 8 7 6 5 4 3 2 1

Printed on acid-free paper

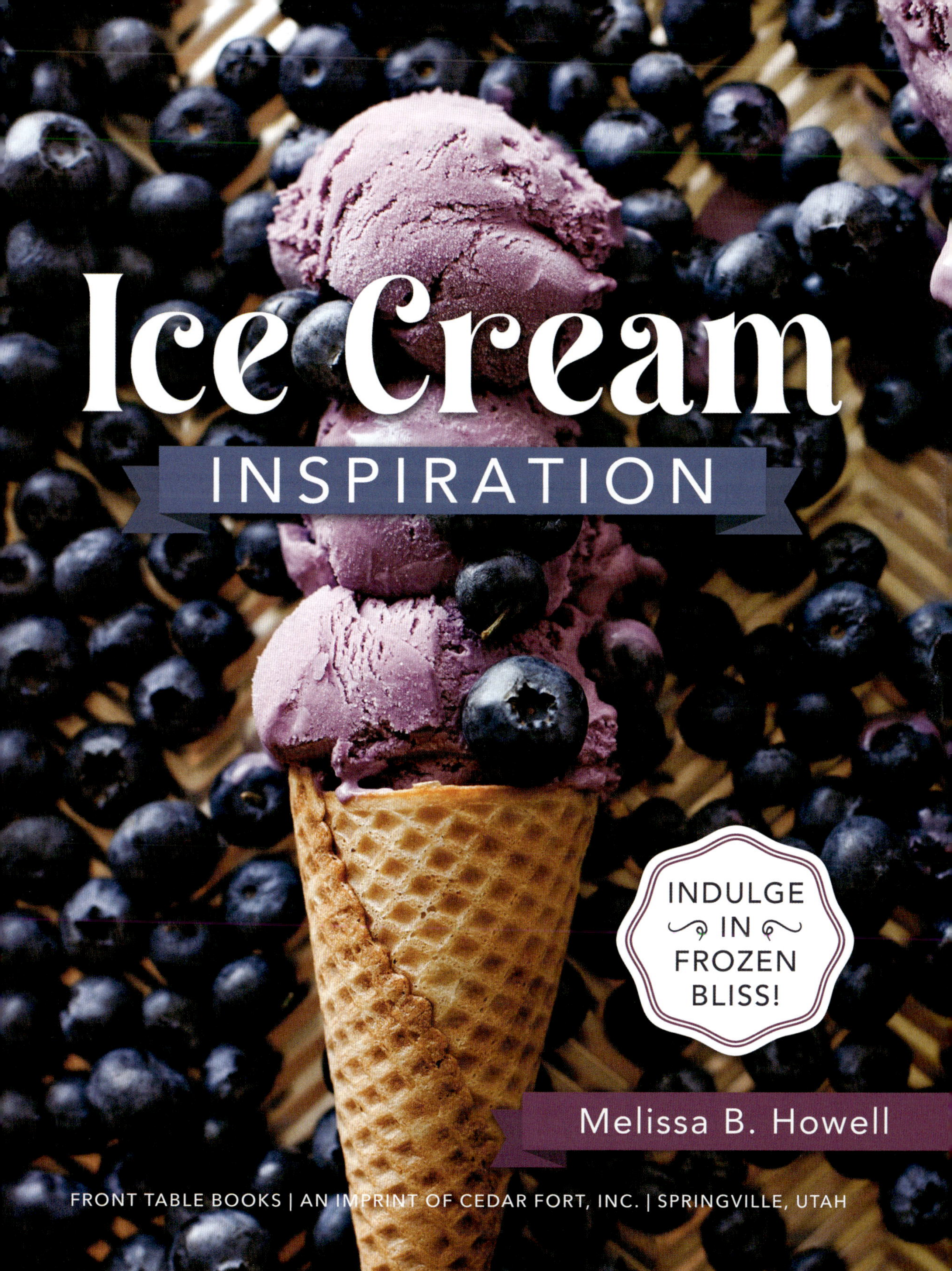
Ice Cream
INSPIRATION
INDULGE
IN
FROZEN
BLISS!
Melissa B. Howell
FRONT TABLE BOOKS | AN IMPRINT OF CEDAR FORT, INC. | SPRINGVILLE, UTAH

CONTENTS

FRUITY ICE CREAM FLAVORS | 43

PIE AND CHEESECAKE ICE CREAM FLAVORS | 67

ADD-INS AND TOPPINGS | 117

INTRODUCTION

Could ice cream bring about world peace? I don't know. But I bet that if you got two opposing world leaders together at a lovely café and gave them each a big bowl of ice cream, peace talks would go a lot better.

Even though ice cream hasn't been used to stop wars, it has been used for almost every other event in our personal lives. You want to celebrate your son's little league win? Go out for ice cream! It's your daughter's birthday? Bring out the ice cream! Your boyfriend dumped you? Time to spend some quality time with a spoon and a whole carton of Rocky Road while sitting on the couch and bingeing your favorite show all night.

Today, making ice cream at home is easier than ever thanks to ice cream makers that don't involve ice, salt, and a hand crank. But some ice cream recipes involve a lot of steps before you can even start churning your ice cream. In other words, they take a lot of time and effort.

I'm here to change all that so you can eat your delicious homemade ice cream as soon as possible!

Here's how my recipes are different:

NO EGGS: None of my ice cream recipes use eggs. This is great news if you're allergic to eggs! It's also great news if you're allergic to the extra work it takes to heat your milk, temper your eggs, strain your custard mixture, and then wait hours and hours for it to cool.

NO COOKING YOUR ICE CREAM BASE: In addition to tempering eggs and making a custard base, some recipes call for you to cook your base, then transfer it to a plastic bag and plunge it into an ice bath. There is none of that here. (No offense to people who like plunging things into ice baths).

NO HARD-TO-FIND OR UNUSUAL INGREDIENTS: Many other ice cream cookbooks are filled with creative, super exotic ice cream flavors. There's only one problem—I'm guessing you don't have access to that special fruit grown in a certain valley in the south of France that is available only one weekend a year at a farmer's market in Wisconsin!

Additionally, it's really awesome that some of these recipe developers and chefs figured out how to put salmon in ice cream, but I don't want to have any part of it! Same goes for broccoli! I'm all for getting kids to eat their vegetables, but I think even kids would balk at asparagus ice cream.

All the ingredients in my ice cream recipes are delicious, actually belong in ice cream, and are probably in your kitchen right now. And if they're not, a quick trip to the local supermarket will give you access to everything you need.

Making ice cream has never been quicker and easier. Guaranteed!

WHY ICE CREAM, AND WHY ME?

The year was 2014. I was walking through Costco with my husband and we noticed a Cuisinart Ice Cream Maker on sale. I'd never made ice cream before in my life. In fact, I thought of ice cream as a "lesser dessert"—nothing to get excited about.

All that changed (drastically!) with the purchase of that ice cream maker. I quickly became obsessed with making ice cream. I started my own blog called Ice Cream Inspiration (now called Beautiful Life and Home) and began posting ice cream recipes.

I thought about ice cream constantly. I dreamed about new flavors and made hundreds of batches of ice cream, testing out ingredients, proportions, and add-ins. I had ice cream tasting parties where my friends gave me feedback on my ice cream, and also helped clean out my freezer so I could make more.

Some of my ice cream recipes top the Google rankings. But what I love most is when readers write to tell me how delicious my ice cream is, share their own ice cream making secrets, or tell me that they use my recipe for Vanilla Spice Ice Cream in their ice cream shop and their customers love it!

I'm not a classically trained chef. I'm just a normal person who happens to be obsessed with ice cream. I experiment over and over again until I get just the right balance of flavors and texture. I don't quit until I get it right.

When I began my blog, I had a dream of one day writing an ice cream book called *Ice Cream Inspiration*. I wanted it to be filled with ice cream recipes that were easy to make for adults and kids alike.

This is that book.

I hope my ice cream recipes will add to your joy and happiness, even though they may also add to your waistline. Sorry about that!

Enjoy,

Melissa

ICE CREAM CHEMISTRY 101

Don't worry—there's no test. In fact, this is the easiest chemistry class you'll ever take.

The flavor and texture of ice cream is determined by the interplay between four main components: sugar, water, fat, and air. Getting these four things in the right proportions is the key to having delicious, creamy ice cream. Let's talk briefly about each one.

SUGAR: Sugar is essential for ice cream, not just for the taste, but also for the texture. Besides its obvious sweetening properties, it also acts as an anti-freezing agent. Too little sugar, and your ice cream will be hard when frozen. Too much sugar, and your ice cream will never quite firm up in the freezer.

WATER: You might be thinking, "Water? What is she talking about? There's no water in ice cream!" Surprisingly, there is. When you consider that milk contains a lot of water, you'll realize quickly that the amount of milk (and the type you use) affects the amount of water in your ice cream. Additionally, fruits contain varying concentrations of water, which also affects the texture of your ice cream. Getting the water ratio right, or mitigating it with other ingredients that bind to the water, is essential. Otherwise, you'll have hard, crumbly ice cream. It will still taste good—it just won't have the perfect texture.

FAT: Heavy whipping cream is the largest component of ice cream. It provides the majority of the fat in the ice cream. It's also what makes ice cream so, well, creamy. But if you have too much fat in your ice cream, it can become dense and overly butter-like in its texture.

AIR: Did you know that the U.S. government regulates how much air can be in ice cream? In order to be considered "ice cream," a frozen confection can be comprised of up to 50% air! Yep. That means that all that cheap ice cream you've been buying at the store is cheap for a reason. You're paying for air. Once you start making ice cream at home, you'll quickly notice that the store-bought variety (even many of the premium, expensive brands) are a lot "fluffier" than what you make at home. Your ice cream maker is designed to incorporate the proper amount of air into your ice cream so that it will have a smooth, creamy texture. Just allow your ice cream maker to run until the ice cream stops churning, and you'll have perfectly aerated ice cream.

SUPPLIES YOU WILL NEED

You only need a few simple tools to make the best ice cream you've ever had.

AN ICE CREAM MAKER: All the recipes in this book require the use of an ice cream maker. Thankfully, there are consumer-grade models that are affordable and easy to use.

I've purchased several ice cream makers and tested them out to see which one works the best. My hands-down favorite ice cream maker is The *Cuisinart 1.5 Quart Frozen Yogurt, Ice Cream and Sorbet Maker.*

This ice cream maker comes with an insulated freezer bowl that you keep in your freezer until you're ready to make your ice cream. It also includes a dasher (a plastic piece that aerates your ice cream) and a motor base that spins the freezer bowl.

I've been making ice cream with this ice cream maker for years. It's my favorite because it makes ice cream faster than any other model I've tried (even a fancy, expensive ice cream maker with a compressor) and you can get extra bowls to keep in your freezer so you can make successive batches of ice cream.

All the recipes in this book are designed to make 1.5 quarts of ice cream (with a few exceptions), which fits perfectly in this machine.

AIRTIGHT CONTAINERS FOR STORING YOUR ICE CREAM: You can use any type of airtight container for storing you ice cream, such as plastic food storage containers, or even gallon-sized zip-top bags in a pinch. However, if you're serious about making ice cream (and I think you are), you're going to want to get dedicated ice cream storage containers. My favorite brand is The *Tovolo Glide-A-Scoop, Non-Slip Base, Insulated Ice Cream Tub, 1.5 Quart.*

These ice cream tubs are oblong and perfectly guide your ice cream scoop. They hold a standard 1.5 quart of ice cream, and are narrow enough to fit into tight spaces in your freezer.

A WIRE WHISK: A wire whisk is ideal for mixing together the ingredients for your ice cream base. You don't want to use an electric hand mixer, or you could splatter milk and cream all over your kitchen.

A BLENDER: Some ice cream recipes, and most sorbet recipes, require the use of a blender. Especially when you're puréeing fruit, a blender (or food processor) is a must.

A SMALL RUBBER SCRAPER: Why should it be small, you ask? The dasher (the plastic removable part of the ice cream maker that aerates your ice cream) is configured with several angles and sloping planes. At the end of your churning cycle, your ice cream will usually be stuck on it, and you'll need to get all that delicious ice cream out of the crevices of the dasher and into your airtight container. Having a small rubber scraper nearby is super handy for this task.

A SLANTED OR FLAT-BOTTOMED WOODEN SPOON: When your ice cream is done churning, some will be stuck to the bottom and sides of the freezer bowl. A rubber scraper is not strong enough to get it off. Metal utensils may dent or scratch the inside of the bowl. A slanted or flat-bottomed wooden spoon is ideal, as it will not injure your bowl, is stiff enough not to break, and helps grab all the ice cream on the bottom and sides of the bowl.

ESSENTIAL ICE CREAM INGREDIENTS

Now that you know all about the chemistry of ice cream, let's briefly discuss the specific ingredients needed for ice cream.

MILK: When making ice cream, use whole milk—not 1% or 2%, and for heaven's sake, not skim milk. Anything other than whole milk contains too much water and will cause your ice cream to be crumbly.

A WORD ABOUT MILK ALTERNATIVES: If you want to make ice cream with non-dairy milk, such as soy milk, almond milk, oat milk, etc., you need to keep in mind two essential things: these types of milk have a high water content and a low fat content. This means that your ice cream will likely freeze as hard as a rock once transferred from your ice cream maker and put in the freezer. However, if you plan to eat your ice cream soft-serve, straight from the ice cream maker, feel free to experiment with non-dairy milks.

HEAVY CREAM: Heavy cream (or heavy whipping cream) is between 36% and 40% fat. Don't just get whipping cream, as it has a lower fat content. The cream you buy needs to have the word "heavy" on the carton.

SUGAR: Use regular granulated, caster, or brown sugar in your ice cream. If you want to use sugar with larger crystals (such as turbinado sugar), make sure to pulse it in a blender or food processor first. Otherwise, the crystals may not fully dissolve in your ice cream base, and you'll end up with gritty ice cream.

Some of my recipes call for a small amount of light corn syrup (not to be confused with high-fructose corn syrup, which is used in commercial products and not generally available for purchase). Corn syrup can be especially helpful in sorbets and ice creams with fruit and other high-water-content ingredients, because it binds with the water and helps maintain the creamy texture of the ice cream.

A WORD ABOUT SUGAR ALTERNATIVES: If you want to use "natural" sugars such as honey, agave, or maple syrup, keep in mind two things: these natural sugars are often sweeter than granulated sugar, and they also have a high water content. This will affect the flavor and texture of your ice cream.

Sugar substitutes, like stevia (often sold in small packets), xylitol, or monk fruit sweetener, alter the texture of your ice cream due to their different chemical properties:

Using stevia will cause your ice cream to freeze extremely hard.

Xylitol or monk fruit sweetener (which also contains erythritol) will give you the opposite problem—your ice cream will never firm up, even after being frozen for hours or days. You can still use these sugar substitutes if you plan to eat your ice cream soft-serve, right after churning.

If using sugar substitutes, also make sure to compensate for their differing sweetness levels. Some things have a 1:1 substitution (like one cup of monk fruit sweetener for one cup of sugar). Other things have a different ratio (like only one teaspoon of stevia for one cup of sugar, depending on the brand you buy).

I do not recommend using sugar substitutes such as aspartame, saccharine, or sucralose.

FLAVORINGS: You can use many different things to flavor ice creams, from chocolate, to spices, to extracts. My favorite way to flavor ice cream is with pure essential oils. You can use flavor extracts, but pure essential oils give a cleaner, punchier flavor. If you use essential oils, be sure they are approved for internal use. I use dōTERRA® essential oils.

FRUITS: For most recipes that call for fruit, you can use either fresh or frozen fruit. This is particularly true when you are making a sorbet, or when you're making a berry purée. Adding chopped fresh fruit like strawberries to ice cream requires a little extra care and preparation so the fruit doesn't get hard and icy. (See my recipe for Strawberry Ice Cream on page 26).

ADD-INS: The sky is the limit here! You can use your imagination to add all kinds of things to ice cream, like broken cookies or candy bars, brownies, nuts, and so much more! When adding things to your ice cream, consider how hard they will be when frozen. You don't want to break your tooth on a surprise "rock" in your ice cream!

COOL TIPS FOR AMAZING ICE CREAM

Here are some helpful hints to make sure your ice cream turns out perfect, every time!

1. DON'T OVER-FILL YOUR ICE CREAM MAKER.

Most of my recipes make 1.5 quarts of ice cream. Check the capacity of your ice cream maker to make sure it can handle this amount. If not, you'll need to churn your ice cream in two batches. If using an ice cream maker with a freezer bowl, you can churn two successive batches of ice cream in the same bowl. The second batch will just take longer because the bowl won't be as cold.

A few of my recipes may overflow if added all at once to your ice cream maker. For these recipes, you'll always see a suggestion to churn in two batches.

As a general rule, don't fill your freezer bowl above two-thirds of its capacity. It's better to churn a small second batch than to overfill your ice cream maker, cross your fingers, and hope it doesn't overflow!

2. STORE YOUR FREEZER BOWL AT THE BACK OF YOUR FREEZER.

The back of the freezer is the coldest, best place for your freezer bowl. The colder your bowl, the faster your ice cream will be ready.

Make sure to leave your freezer bowl in your freezer until right before you start churning your ice cream. Ideally, you should have your ice cream base poured into your freezer bowl and ready to churn within one minute of removing your freezer bowl from the freezer.

3. KNOW WHEN YOUR ICE CREAM IS DONE CHURNING.

This is pretty easy to figure out. When your ice cream is all stuck to your dasher and is no longer moving, it's done! If your ice cream never gets to this point, it may be because your ice cream bowl wasn't cold enough, or because you over-filled your bowl. If your ice cream starts overflowing, you can either remove some and keep churning, or just transfer it all to your ice cream container and put it in the freezer right away.

4. GET YOUR CHURNED ICE CREAM INTO THE FREEZER AS FAST AS POSSIBLE.

When you transfer your ice cream into your airtight container, get it into the freezer as soon as you can. The faster ice cream freezes, the better the texture will be, because fewer ice crystals will form in your ice cream.

If you need to churn your ice cream in two batches, transfer the first batch to an airtight container and place it in the freezer while you churn the second batch. Then you can remove the first batch from the freezer briefly while you add the second batch on top.

If desired, you can place a piece of plastic wrap directly over the top of the ice cream and press it lightly into the ice cream to keep ice crystals from forming on the surface. Then cover with your lid and place in the freezer.

5. ALLOW THE ICE CREAM TO SIT AT ROOM TEMPERATURE FOR 10 MINUTES BEFORE SERVING.

Your homemade ice cream may be more difficult to scoop than store-bought ice cream. This is because less air has been whipped into your ice cream, making it more dense and creamy. Just let it sit for 10 minutes at room temperature before scooping. Don't worry about it melting. Cold temperatures mute the flavors of ice cream, so if your ice cream starts to get a little soft, it will taste even better!

6. PLAN AHEAD.

Many recipes can be made in just 30 minutes and be eaten soft-serve. Some recipes take longer because they require chilling your ice cream base before churning, or the preparation of add-ins.

Be aware that churning time can be affected by the temperature of your ice cream base and the temperature of your ice cream bowl, so it may take longer (or less) than 30 minutes. Also keep in mind that if you want your ice cream to be firm, you'll need to chill it after churning for at least 4 hours. Your best bet is to make any ice cream at least a day before you plan on serving it.

O.K.! I think you're more than ready to make ice cream now, so let's get to the recipes!

Classic
ICE CREAM FLAVORS

With these basic flavors in your back pocket, you can mix and match to create endless flavors!

Classic Vanilla

You'll soon have this recipe memorized!
What's better than soft-serve vanilla ice cream in only 30 minutes?

INGREDIENTS:

¾ cup granulated sugar

1 cup whole milk

2 cups heavy cream

1–2 tsp. pure vanilla extract, to taste

INSTRUCTIONS:

1. In a medium bowl, use a whisk to combine the milk and sugar until the sugar is dissolved.
2. Add the heavy cream and vanilla and mix well.
3. Pour into your ice cream maker and follow the manufacturer's directions.
4. Transfer to an airtight container and freeze for 4 hours or overnight.

· FLAVOR VARIATIONS ·

COOKIES AND CREAM

1. Break up 10 chocolate sandwich cookies by hand. (Chopping the cookies in a food processor will create too many crumbs and make your ice cream sandy.)
2. Transfer your Classic Vanilla Ice Cream in layers into your airtight container, dropping the broken cookies on top of each layer.

STRACCIATELLA

1. Melt ¼ cup semi-sweet or dark chocolate chips. During the last few minutes of churning, pour a thin drizzle of melted chocolate through the opening at the top of your ice cream machine. The chocolate will freeze on contact and break into little pieces as it is churned throughout the ice cream.
2. Alternately, you can grate 2 ounces of a chocolate candy bar and add the grated chocolate during the last few minutes of churning.

FUDGE RIPPLE

1. Drizzle Hot Fudge Sauce (pg. 132) in layers over the ice cream as you transfer it to an airtight container. It's best if the Hot Fudge Sauce is at room temperature or just slightly warmer so that it doesn't melt your ice cream.

CARAMEL SWIRL

1. Drizzle Caramel Sauce (pg. 127) in layers over the ice cream as you transfer it to an airtight container.

Classic Chocolate

This is the perfect base for many ice cream flavors. Switch things up by using different types of chocolate chips and add-ins for endless variety.

INGREDIENTS:

½ cup granulated sugar

8 ounces (slightly more than 1 cup) semi-sweet or dark chocolate chips

1 cup whole milk

2 cups heavy cream

1 tsp. pure vanilla extract

INSTRUCTIONS:

1. Add the granulated sugar and chocolate chips to a blender. Pulse until the chocolate is very finely chopped.
2. Heat the whole milk in a small saucepan on the stove over medium heat until just bubbling around the edges.
3. Add the hot milk to the chocolate and sugar in the blender and process until smooth.
4. Put in your refrigerator to chill for at least 2 hours.
5. When ready to churn your ice cream, add the heavy cream and vanilla to your chocolate mixture and mix well.
6. Pour into your ice cream maker and follow the manufacturer's directions.
7. Transfer to an airtight container and freeze for 4 hours or overnight.

· FLAVOR VARIATIONS ·

CHOCOLATE COOKIES AND CREAM

1. Break up 10 chocolate sandwich cookies by hand. (Chopping the cookies in a food processor will create too many crumbs and make your ice cream sandy.)
2. Transfer your Classic Chocolate Ice Cream in layers into your airtight container, dropping the broken cookies on top of each layer.

CHOCOLATE MINT

1. Add 15 drops of peppermint essential oil to your ice cream base before churning. If using peppermint extract, use 1–2 teaspoons, to taste.

CHOCOLATE FUDGE RIPPLE

1. Drizzle Hot Fudge Sauce (pg. 132) in layers over the ice cream as you transfer it to an airtight container. It's best if the Hot Fudge Sauce is at room temperature or just slightly warmer so that it doesn't melt your ice cream.

CHOCOLATE ORANGE

1. Add 10 drops of orange essential oil, or 1 teaspoon orange extract to your ice cream base before churning. If desired, drop spoonfuls of orange marmalade into your ice cream as you transfer it in layers to an airtight container. Slightly swirl the ice cream to break up the spoonfuls of marmalade.

CHOCOLATE PEANUT BUTTER COOKIE DOUGH

1. Add small balls of Peanut Butter Cookie Dough (pg. 123) into your ice cream in layers as you transfer it to your airtight container.

Strawberry

Real strawberries are the star of this ice cream. The natural strawberry juice makes it a lovely pale pink, but you can amp up the color by adding red food coloring if desired.

INGREDIENTS:

2 cups fresh strawberries, hulled and chopped
1 Tbsp. fresh lemon juice
⅔ cup granulated sugar, divided
⅓ cup light corn syrup
1 cup whole milk
2 cups heavy cream
1 tsp. pure vanilla extract
1–2 drops red food coloring, optional

INSTRUCTIONS:

1. Add the chopped strawberries (and any juices released while chopping), the lemon juice, and ⅓ cup of granulated sugar to a small bowl. Leave on the counter for 2 hours. The strawberries will release their juices and absorb some of the sugar. (This will lower their freezing point so they don't turn into rocks in your ice cream.)
2. In a separate medium-sized mixing bowl, mix the remaining ⅓ cup granulated sugar with the ⅓ cup light corn syrup and 1 cup of whole milk. Whisk until the sugar is dissolved.
3. Add the heavy cream and vanilla.
4. Pour in the liquid from the strawberries, saving the strawberries to add later.
5. Add red food coloring if desired.
6. Pour into your ice cream maker and follow the manufacturer's directions.
7. When the ice cream has reached soft-serve consistency, add the chopped strawberries and let the ice cream machine continue churning for another 1–2 minutes, until the strawberries have been evenly distributed throughout the ice cream.
8. Transfer to an airtight container and freeze for 4 hours or overnight.

• FLAVOR VARIATION •

STRAWBERRY WHITE (OR DARK) CHOCOLATE SWIRL

1. Melt ¼ cup of white (or dark) chocolate chips.
2. Drizzle the melted chocolate over the ice cream in layers as you transfer it to your airtight container.

Mint

There's nothing more disappointing than mint ice cream that is green, but barely tastes like mint! This recipe fixes all that, with the punchiest mint flavor you've ever had in ice cream!

INGREDIENTS:

¾ cup granulated sugar
1 cup whole milk
2 cups heavy cream
15 drops dōTERRA® peppermint essential oil, or 1–2 tsp. peppermint extract, to taste
2 drops green food coloring, optional

INSTRUCTIONS:

1. In a medium bowl, use a whisk to combine the milk and sugar until the sugar is dissolved.
2. Add the heavy cream and peppermint essential oil or peppermint extract and mix well.
3. Pour into your ice cream maker and follow the manufacturer's directions.
4. Transfer to an airtight container and freeze for 4 hours or overnight.

• FLAVOR VARIATIONS •

MINT COOKIES AND CREAM

1. Break up 10 chocolate sandwich cookies by hand. (Chopping the cookies in a food processor will create too many crumbs and make your ice cream sandy.)
2. Transfer your Mint Ice Cream in layers into your airtight container, dropping the broken cookies on top of each layer.

MINT CHOCOLATE CHIP

1. Melt ¼ cup semi-sweet or dark chocolate chips. During the last few minutes of churning, pour a thin drizzle of melted chocolate through the opening at the top of your ice cream machine. The chocolate will freeze on contact and break into little pieces as it is churned throughout the ice cream.
2. Alternately, you can grate 2 ounces of a chocolate candy bar and add the grated chocolate during the last few minutes of churning.

MINT FUDGE SWIRL

1. Drizzle Hot Fudge Sauce (pg. 132) in layers over the ice cream as you transfer it to an airtight container. It's best if the Hot Fudge Sauce is at room temperature or just slightly warmer so that it doesn't melt your ice cream.

MINT BROWNIE

1. Chop up Decadent Chocolate Brownies (pg. 119) into bite-sized pieces and drop in layers over the ice cream as you transfer it to an airtight container.

Chocolate Chip Cookie Dough

Feel free to use your own favorite edible chocolate chip cookie dough in this ice cream, or follow my recipe for no-egg Chocolate Chip Cookie Dough. (Try not to eat it all before it makes it into the ice cream!)

INGREDIENTS:

One recipe for Chocolate Chip Cookie Dough (pg. 121)

¾ cup granulated sugar

1 cup whole milk

2 cups heavy cream

1–2 tsp. pure vanilla extract

2 Tbsp. mini chocolate chips

INSTRUCTIONS:

1. Prepare your cookie dough and set aside while you make the ice cream.
2. In a medium bowl, use a whisk to combine the granulated sugar and whole milk until the sugar is dissolved.
3. Add the heavy cream and vanilla and mix well.
4. Pour into your ice cream maker and follow the manufacturer's directions.
5. When ice cream reaches soft-serve consistency, add 2 tablespoons of mini chocolate chips. Let ice cream continue churning until the chocolate chips are evenly distributed throughout.
6. Transfer to an airtight container in layers, dropping balls of the cookie dough on each layer.
7. Freeze for 4 hours or overnight.

Butter Pecan

Roasting the pecans in butter really brings out their signature flavor in this namesake ice cream. It's a classic for a reason!

INGREDIENTS:

¾ cup brown sugar, lightly packed

1 cup whole milk

½ cup chopped pecans

1 Tbsp. salted butter

2 cups heavy cream

INSTRUCTIONS:

1. Heat the whole milk in a microwave-proof bowl for 1 minute. Add the brown sugar and stir until the sugar is dissolved. Chill for at least 1 hour in the refrigerator.
2. While milk and sugar mixture are chilling, add the chopped pecans and butter to a skillet. Heat over medium heat and toast for 5–6 minutes, stirring to coat with butter. Remove from the heat and cool to room temperature.
3. When ready to churn the ice cream, add the heavy cream to the brown sugar/milk mixture and whisk together.
4. Pour into your ice cream maker and follow the manufacturer's directions.
5. When the ice cream reaches soft-serve consistency, add the buttered pecans and continue churning for 1–2 more minutes, until the pecans are evenly distributed throughout the ice cream. Transfer to an airtight container and freeze for 4 hours or overnight.

Pistachio

Don't skip roasting the pistachios! It only takes five minutes but it makes all the difference. This ice cream is best eaten alone so its mild, yet distinctive flavor can really shine.

INGREDIENTS:

⅔ cup shelled, unsalted pistachios

⅔ cup granulated sugar

2 Tbsp. light corn syrup

½ tsp. almond extract

1 cup whole milk

2 cups heavy cream

INSTRUCTIONS:

1. Heat your oven to 350°F.
2. Spread the pistachios on a cookie sheet and roast in the oven for 5 minutes.
3. Remove from the oven and add to a blender. Pulverize until the pistachios turn into a smooth paste. (The paste may look dry and a bit crumbly. That is o.k.)
4. Add the remaining ingredients to the blender with the pistachio paste. Blend on high speed for 45 seconds.
5. Chill for 2 hours.
6. When ready to churn your ice cream, pour your mixture into your ice cream maker and follow the manufacturer's directions. You may need to churn this in two batches.
7. Transfer to an airtight container and freeze for 4 hours or overnight.

Peanut Butter

For all you peanut butter lovers out there, this ice cream is your new best friend! It's got the perfect creamy texture without being too dense.

INGREDIENTS:

1 cup smooth peanut butter (not natural)

1 cup granulated sugar

1 ½ cups whole milk

1 ½ cups heavy cream

¼ tsp. vanilla

INSTRUCTIONS:

1. Add all the ingredients to a blender.
2. Purée on high speed for 45 seconds.
3. Chill for at least 2 hours.
4. Pour into your ice cream maker and follow the manufacturer's directions. You may need to churn this in two batches.
5. Transfer to an airtight container and freeze for 4 hours or overnight.

• FLAVOR VARIATIONS •

PEANUT BUTTER CHOCOLATE FUDGE

1. Drizzle Hot Fudge Sauce (pg. 132) in layers over the ice cream as you transfer it to an airtight container. It's best if the Hot Fudge Sauce is at room temperature or just slightly warmer so that it doesn't melt your ice cream.

PEANUT BUTTER COOKIE

2. Drop broken pieces of peanut butter cookies (like Nutter Butters or homemade peanut butter cookies) in layers over the ice cream as you transfer it to an airtight container. (Break the cookies by hand over a separate bowl so you don't add a lot of cookie crumbs to your ice cream.)

PEANUT BUTTER COOKIE DOUGH

3. Add small balls of Peanut Butter Cookie Dough (pg. 123) or Chocolate Chip Cookie Dough (pg.121) into your ice cream in layers as you transfer it to your airtight container.

PEANUT BUTTER AND JAM

4. Add strawberry jam or grape jelly in layers over the ice cream as you transfer it to an airtight container. Do not stir.

You can never have too much chocolate! Use the recipes in this section as a springboard for your own imaginative chocolate ice cream flavors!

Mexican Chocolate

This ice cream has a deep chocolate flavor enhanced with cinnamon and a sneaky kick of cayenne at the end of every bite.

INGREDIENTS:

2 cups whole milk, divided

1 tablet Nestle's Abuelita Mexican Chocolate (found in most supermarkets in the Mexican section—see note below)

¾ cup granulated sugar

1 tsp. pure vanilla extract

¼ cup unsweetened cocoa powder (not hot chocolate powder)

1 tsp. ground cinnamon

⅛ tsp. cayenne pepper

2 cups heavy whipping cream

Note: If you can only find granulated Mexican chocolate drink mix, use 1 cup of whole milk and double the amount of powder specified in the instructions on the package.

INSTRUCTIONS:

1. Pour 2 cups of whole milk into a small pot on the stove. Add the tablet of Mexican chocolate and heat over medium heat. Gently stir until the tablet is melted.
2. Add the granulated sugar to a large mixing bowl.
3. Pour 1 cup of the Mexican hot chocolate over the sugar and whisk until the sugar is dissolved. (Save the rest of the Mexican hot chocolate for another use. If you want to drink it, add another cup of milk before doing so.)
4. Add the vanilla, cocoa powder, cinnamon, and cayenne pepper. Gently stir until everything is incorporated.
5. Cover and refrigerate for at least 2 hours.
6. When ready to churn, add the heavy cream and mix well.
7. Pour your mixture into your ice cream maker and follow the manufacturer's directions.
8. Transfer to an airtight container and freeze for 4 hours or overnight.

German Chocolate

The best part about German chocolate cake is the frosting, made with coconut, walnuts, and a gooey caramel. Add it to ice cream and the results are pure magic!

INGREDIENTS FOR THE CLASSIC CHOCOLATE ICE CREAM:

½ cup granulated sugar

8 ounces (slightly more than 1 cup) semi-sweet or dark chocolate chips

1 tsp. pure vanilla extract

1 cup whole milk

2 cups heavy cream

INGREDIENTS FOR THE CARAMEL, COCONUT, WALNUT SAUCE:

½ cup jarred or homemade Caramel Sauce (pg. 127)

½ cup shredded coconut, sweetened or unsweetened

½ cup chopped walnuts or pecans

INSTRUCTIONS:

1. Add the granulated sugar and chocolate chips to a blender. Pulse until the chocolate is very finely chopped.
2. Heat the whole milk in a small saucepan on the stove until just bubbling around the edges.
3. Add the hot milk to the chocolate and sugar in the blender and process until smooth.
4. Put in your refrigerator to chill for at least 2 hours.
5. While your ice cream base is chilling, prepare your Caramel, Coconut, Walnut Sauce by mixing together the caramel sauce, coconut, and chopped walnuts or pecans. Set aside at room temperature.
6. When ready to churn your ice cream, add the heavy cream and vanilla to your chocolate mixture and mix well.
7. Pour into your ice cream maker and follow the manufacturer's directions.
8. Transfer to an airtight container in layers, dropping spoonfuls of the Caramel, Coconut, Walnut sauce on each layer. Do not stir.
9. Freeze for 4 hours or overnight.

Chocolate Caramel Toffee

If you're an English toffee lover like me, this ice cream will be pure heaven! Use your own recipe for English toffee, or buy toffee bits next to the chocolate chips at the store.

INGREDIENTS:

½ cup granulated sugar

8 ounces (slightly more than 1 cup) semi-sweet or dark chocolate chips

1 tsp. pure vanilla extract

1 cup whole milk

2 cups heavy cream

¼ cup jarred or homemade Caramel Sauce (pg. 127)

¼ cup small toffee pieces

INSTRUCTIONS:

1. Add the granulated sugar and chocolate chips to a blender. Pulse until the chocolate is very finely chopped.
2. Heat the whole milk in a small saucepan on the stove until just bubbling around the edges.
3. Add the hot milk to the chocolate and sugar in the blender and process until smooth.
4. Put in your refrigerator to chill for at least 2 hours.
5. If using homemade Caramel Sauce, make it while the ice cream base is chilling. Allow the Caramel Sauce to come to room temperature.
6. When ready to churn your ice cream, add the heavy cream and vanilla to your chocolate mixture and mix well.
7. Pour into your ice cream maker and follow the manufacturer's directions.
8. Transfer to an airtight container in layers, drizzling caramel sauce on each layer, and dropping the toffee pieces on top of each layer. Do not stir.
9. Freeze for 4 hours or overnight.

Chocolate Brownie Chunk

This ice cream is the perfect way to use up leftover brownies!
(What are "leftover brownies?" Is that even a thing?)
O.K. You might have to make some brownies. That's not a problem, is it?
Check out my recipe for Decadent Chocolate Brownies on pg. 119.

INGREDIENTS:

½ cup granulated sugar

8 ounces (slightly more than 1 cup) semi-sweet or dark chocolate chips

1 tsp. pure vanilla extract

1 cup whole milk

2 cups heavy cream

3 or 4 large day-old chocolate brownies, cut into bite-sized pieces

INSTRUCTIONS:

1. Add the sugar and chocolate chips to a blender. Pulse until the chocolate is finely chopped.
2. Heat the whole milk in a small saucepan on the stove until just bubbling around the edges.
3. Add the hot milk to the chocolate and sugar in the blender and process until smooth.
4. Put in your refrigerator to chill for at least 2 hours.
5. When ready to churn your ice cream, add the heavy cream and vanilla to your chocolate mixture and mix well.
6. Pour into your ice cream maker and follow the manufacturer's directions.
7. Transfer to an airtight container in layers, dropping chopped brownies on each layer. Do not stir. Freeze for 4 hours or overnight.

Dark Chocolate Raspberry Swirl

Sophisticated and rich, this ice cream is the perfect dessert after a fancy meal.

INGREDIENTS:

¾ cup granulated sugar

8 ounces (slightly more than 1 cup) dark chocolate chips

1 cup whole milk

2 cups heavy cream

1 tsp. pure vanilla extract

½ cup Berry Topping for Ice Cream (pg. 134, use only raspberries in the recipe) or ½ cup raspberry jam

INSTRUCTIONS:

1. Add the granulated sugar and chocolate chips to a blender. Pulse until the chocolate is very finely chopped.
2. Heat the whole milk in a small saucepan on the stove until just bubbling around the edges.
3. Add the hot milk to the chocolate and sugar in the blender and process until smooth.
4. Put in your refrigerator to chill for at least 2 hours.
5. If making Berry Topping for Ice Cream, make it while the ice cream base is chilling. Cool to room temperature or refrigerate.
6. When ready to churn your ice cream, add the heavy cream and vanilla to your chocolate mixture and mix well.
7. Pour into your ice cream maker and follow the manufacturer's directions.
8. Transfer to an airtight container in layers, adding in the raspberry topping or raspberry jam. If desired, gently fold the ice cream or swirl it in a figure-eight to distribute the raspberry topping or jam. Don't over-stir.

Rocky Road

Use marshmallow crème instead of the traditional marshmallows in this ice cream. The crème will stay soft, even when frozen.

INGREDIENTS:

½ cup granulated sugar
8 ounces (slightly more than 1 cup) semi-sweet or dark chocolate chips
1 tsp. pure vanilla extract
1 tsp. almond extract
1 cup whole milk
2 cups heavy cream
½ cup whole almonds (raw, or roasted and unsalted)

INSTRUCTIONS:

1. Add the granulated sugar and chocolate chips to a blender. Pulse until the chocolate is very finely chopped.
2. Heat the whole milk in a small saucepan on the stove until just bubbling around the edges.
3. Add the hot milk to the chocolate and sugar in the blender and process until smooth.
4. Put in your refrigerator to chill for at least 2 hours.
5. While ice cream base is chilling, roast your almonds (unless using almonds that have already been roasted). Heat your oven to 350°F. Add whole, raw almonds to a small baking sheet and roast for 7–8 minutes, until fragrant.
6. Remove from the oven and transfer to a blender or food processor. Cool for at least 30 minutes.
7. When almonds have cooled a little (or if using already roasted almonds), pulse a few times in the blender until coarsely chopped. Set aside.
8. When ready to churn your ice cream, add the heavy cream and vanilla to your chocolate mixture and mix well.
9. Pour into your ice cream maker and follow the manufacturer's directions.
10. When ice cream has reached soft-serve consistency, add the chopped almonds and allow ice cream to churn 1 or 2 more minutes until the almonds are evenly distributed.
11. Transfer to an airtight container, dropping dollops of marshmallow crème on each layer.
12. Freeze for 4 hours or overnight.

• FLAVOR VARIATION •

BURNT ALMOND FUDGE

1. Omit the marshmallow crème. For more chocolate flavor, add layers of Chocolate Sauce (pg. 131) or Hot Fudge Sauce (pg. 132) while transferring to an airtight container.

Fresh fruit and essential oils bring these ice cream flavors to life! If you don't have fresh fruit on hand, frozen fruit works just as well. You can enjoy fruity ice cream any time of the year!

Blueberry

One of the most gorgeous ice creams you will ever make!
Its deep purple color is stunning, and so is its flavor!

INGREDIENTS:

1 ½ cups fresh or frozen blueberries

1 cup plus 2 Tbsp. granulated sugar, divided

1 Tbsp. lemon juice

1 cup whole milk

2 cups heavy cream

INSTRUCTIONS:

1. Start by making a thick blueberry syrup. Combine the blueberries, ½ cup of sugar, and the lemon juice in a small saucepan.
2. Heat over medium heat for about 5 minutes, until the blueberries soften and begin to break down.
3. Remove from the stove and purée in a blender.
4. Pour through a mesh sieve to remove the seeds. (Some of the seeds may still get through. That is o.k.)
5. Return the blueberry mixture to the pan on the stove and cook over medium heat, stirring constantly, until most of the liquid has evaporated and the mixture has thickened (about 15 minutes).
6. Transfer the blueberry mixture to a small container and place in the refrigerator for at least 2 hours or overnight.
7. When fully chilled, the mixture will look like thick jelly.
8. When ready to churn your ice cream, add the chilled blueberry mixture, along with ½ cup plus 2 tablespoons of sugar to a large mixing bowl. Stir together.
9. Add 1 cup of whole milk and whisk together until all the lumps are gone.
10. Add 2 cups of heavy whipping cream and whisk together.
11. Pour into your ice cream maker and follow the manufacturer's directions.
12. When ice cream has reached soft-serve consistency, transfer to an airtight container and freeze for 4 hours or overnight.

Black Cherry

Save yourself the trouble of pitting fresh cherries and use frozen, pitted cherries instead. You'll save a boatload of time and keep your hands and clothes from getting stained with cherry juice.

INGREDIENTS:

3 cups fresh or frozen black cherries, pitted

1 cup granulated sugar, divided

3 Tbsp. light corn syrup

2 Tbsp. lemon juice

1 cup whole milk

2 cups heavy cream

1 tsp. vanilla extract

INSTRUCTIONS:

1. Chop your cherries in a food processor or blender by pulsing until finely chopped (not puréed).
2. Add the chopped cherries to a medium-sized bowl with ⅓ cup of sugar and the lemon juice. Stir and allow to sit at room temperature on your counter for 1-2 hours. This will draw the juices out of the cherries.
3. When almost ready to churn, prepare the ice cream mixture by adding the remaining ⅔ cup of sugar, corn syrup, and whole milk to a large mixing bowl. Whisk until the sugar has dissolved.
4. Add the heavy whipping cream and vanilla extract to the milk and sugar and blend well.
5. Carefully add the cherries and all their juices to the ice cream mixture. Stir until everything is well-blended.
6. Add to your ice cream maker and follow the manufacturer's instructions. Depending on the size of your ice cream maker, you may need to churn this in 2 batches.
7. Transfer to an airtight container and freeze for 4 hours or overnight.

Cherry Chocolate

You can't beat this gorgeous pink ice cream with pieces of maraschino cherries and flecks of chocolate!

INGREDIENTS:

⅓ cup maraschino cherry juice (from a jar of maraschino cherries)

⅔ cup granulated sugar

1 cup whole milk

2 cups heavy cream

1 tsp. almond extract

½ tsp. cherry extract (optional)

1 cup coarsely chopped maraschino cherries

2 ounces dark chocolate, grated

INSTRUCTIONS:

1. Mix together the maraschino cherry juice and sugar in a large mixing bowl.
2. Add the milk and blend.
3. Add the heavy cream, almond extract, and cherry extract (optional).
4. Pour into your ice cream maker and follow the manufacturer's directions.
5. A few minutes before the ice cream is done churning, add the chopped cherries and grated chocolate. Continue churning until cherries and chocolate are evenly distributed throughout.
6. Transfer to an airtight container and freeze for 4 hours or overnight.
7. Tip: Use a coarse grater, not a microplane (for zesting) to grate the chocolate. Otherwise, the chocolate becomes full of static electricity and tiny pieces stick to everything!
8. Alternately, you can drizzle melted chocolate over the ice cream during the last few minutes of churning.

• FLAVOR VARIATION •

CHERRY CHOCOLATE FUDGE

1. Leave out the grated chocolate. Add small scoops of chilled Hot Fudge Sauce (pg. 132) in layers as you transfer your ice cream to your airtight container.

Strawberry Pretzel

Sweet strawberry ice cream with a slightly buttery, salty pretzel crust. It's a flavor combination made in heaven!

INGREDIENTS:

One recipe for Pretzel Topping (pg. 139)

1 cup fresh or frozen strawberries, thawed

3 oz. package of strawberry flavored gelatin (about ½ cup gelatin powder)

1 cup whole milk

2 cups heavy cream

½ cup sugar

1 tsp. pure vanilla extract

INSTRUCTIONS:

1. Make the Pretzel Topping. Cool completely.
2. Purée the strawberries in a blender.
3. Pour the blended strawberries into a large mixing bowl and add the sugar and strawberry gelatin. Mix well.
4. Add the whole milk and vanilla and mix with a wire whisk until everything is blended.
5. Add the heavy cream and mix well.
6. Pour into your ice cream maker and follow the manufacturer's directions.
7. When ice cream reaches soft-serve consistency, transfer to an airtight container, layering with pieces of the pretzel crust. (You may not use all the pretzel crust, depending on your personal preference.)
8. Freeze for 4 hours or overnight.

Peaches and Cream

This classic flavor has been found at family reunions and summertime parties since our grandparents' days.

INGREDIENTS:

2 cups peeled, chopped peaches (about three peaches)

1 ¼ cups sugar, divided

3 Tbsp. light corn syrup

1 cup whole milk

2 cups heavy cream

1 tsp. pure vanilla extract

INSTRUCTIONS:

1. Add the chopped peaches to a blender along with ¼ cup of the sugar. Pulse 2 or 3 times to distribute the sugar throughout the peaches. Allow to sit at room temperature for 30 minutes. The sugar will draw the juices out of the peaches.
2. After 30 minutes, add the remaining cup of sugar, light corn syrup, and cup of milk to the blender. Blend on high speed for 30 seconds.
3. Add the heavy cream and vanilla and blend for 30 more seconds.
4. Refrigerate for at least 2 hours.
5. Pour into your ice cream maker and follow the manufacturer's directions. You will need to churn this in 2 batches.

Orange White Chocolate Macadamia Nut

This flavor was inspired by the super delicious white chocolate macadamia nut cookie. I like to add orange essential oil or extract to this ice cream, but you could also add lime zest for another flavor option.

INGREDIENTS:

¾ cup granulated sugar
1 cup whole milk
2 cups heavy cream
1 tsp. pure vanilla extract
15—20 drops of dōTERRA® Wild Orange essential oil or 1–2 tsp. orange extract, to taste
¼ cup white chocolate chips, melted (thinned with ⅛ tsp. vegetable oil, if necessary)
½ cup unsalted, coarsely chopped macadamia nuts

INSTRUCTIONS:

1. Mix milk and sugar with a whisk until sugar is dissolved.
2. Add heavy cream, vanilla, and essential oil or orange extract. Mix well.
3. Pour into your ice cream maker and follow the manufacturer's directions.
4. While ice cream is churning, melt the white chocolate chips over medium-low heat in a saucepan on the stove. Add oil if necessary to thin. Keep warm until ice cream is done churning.
5. When ice cream has reached soft-serve consistency, transfer to an airtight container in layers, drizzling the melted white chocolate and adding macadamia nuts to each layer.
6. Freeze for 4 hours or overnight.

Jungle Nut

Choose bananas with perfectly yellow skins and no brown spots for this recipe.

INGREDIENTS:

⅓ cup white chocolate chips
2 Tbsp. virgin coconut oil
1 tsp. coconut extract
1 tsp. vanilla
1 cup whole milk
2 cups heavy cream
½ cup granulated sugar
2 bananas, coarsely mashed (medium ripe)
½ cup shredded coconut, sweetened or unsweetened
½ cup salted cashews, chopped
⅓ cup chocolate chips, melted

INSTRUCTIONS:

1. Melt the white chocolate chips in a small saucepan over low heat on the stove with the coconut oil.
2. Combine the milk, cream, vanilla, and sugar in a separate pan over low heat. When the sugar has dissolved, add the melted white chocolate chips and coconut oil, and the coconut extract. Mix well.
3. Chill for at least 2 hours.
4. Just before churning, add the mashed bananas and shredded coconut.
5. Pour into your ice cream maker and follow the manufacturer's directions. You may need to churn this in 2 batches.
6. While the ice cream is churning, melt your chocolate chips in a small saucepan on the stove over medium heat, or in the microwave, heating and stirring in 30-second increments.
7. About 1 minute before done churning, add the cashews.
8. When ice cream has reached soft-serve consistency, transfer to an airtight container, drizzling each layer of ice cream with the melted chocolate. Stir if desired to break up the chocolate.
9. Freeze for 4 hours or overnight.

Pear Crumble

This recipe was inspired by a delicious pear crumble dessert. The flavor is delicate and deserves to be enjoyed slowly.

INGREDIENTS:

One recipe for Crumble Topping (pg. 140)

3 large ripe pears

1 Tbsp. butter, salted

¾ cup sugar

¼ cup light corn syrup

1 cup whole milk

2 cups heavy cream

INSTRUCTIONS:

1. Prepare your Crumble Topping and set aside to cool to room temperature.
2. While Crumble Topping is cooling, prepare your ice cream.
3. Peel, core, and slice the pears.
4. Sauté the sliced pears in 1 tablespoon of butter over medium heat in a saucepan on the stove. When pears are softened and almost translucent, transfer to a blender and purée.
5. Pour the purée back into the saucepan. Heat purée on the stove over medium heat, stirring constantly, for about 15 minutes, until as much moisture as possible has evaporated.
6. Pour puréed pears into a large mixing bowl and add the sugar and light corn syrup. Stir until sugar is dissolved. Refrigerate for at least 2 hours.
7. Just before churning, add the milk and heavy whipping cream and mix well. Pour into your ice cream maker and follow the manufacturer's directions.
8. While ice cream is churning, break the Crumble Topping into pieces.
9. Transfer to an airtight container in layers, dropping pieces of the Crumble Topping on each layer. (You may not use all of the crumble topping. You can save any extra crumble topping for garnishing your ice cream when serving).
10. Freeze for 4 hours or overnight.

Banana Split

Here's your banana split, the easy way!
Top with a dollop of whipped cream for the full experience!

INGREDIENTS:

2 cups fresh strawberries, hulled and sliced

1 Tbsp. fresh lemon juice

2 bananas, coarsely mashed (medium ripe)

¼ cup walnuts, chopped

¼ cup dark chocolate chips, melted, or ¼ cup Chocolate Sauce (pg. 131)

⅔ cup granulated sugar, divided

⅓ cup light corn syrup

1 cup whole milk

2 cups heavy cream

1 tsp. pure vanilla extract

1–2 drops red food coloring, optional

INSTRUCTIONS:

1. Combine the sliced strawberries (and any juices released while slicing), the lemon juice, and ⅓ cup of the sugar in a small bowl. Leave on the counter for 2 hours. The strawberries will release their juices and absorb some of the sugar. This will lower their freezing point so they don't turn into rocks in your ice cream!
2. In a separate medium-sized mixing bowl, mix the remaining ⅓ cup of sugar with the light corn syrup and whole milk. Whisk until the sugar is dissolved.
3. Add the heavy cream and vanilla. Pour in the liquid from the strawberries, saving the strawberries to add later. Add food coloring if desired.
4. Pour into your ice cream maker and follow the manufacturer's directions.
5. When the ice cream has reached soft-serve consistency, add the strawberries, mashed bananas, and walnuts, and let the ice cream maker run another minute or two to distribute everything throughout the ice cream.
6. Transfer to an airtight container in layers, drizzling each layer with melted chocolate chips or Chocolate Sauce.
7. Freeze for 4 hours or overnight.
8. Serve with Whipped Cream if desired (pg. 135).

Fresh Lemon

The fresh flavor of lemon is both surprising and delightful in this ice cream with no artificial flavors whatsoever.

INGREDIENTS:

3 lemons, washed

1 cup plus 2 Tbsp. granulated sugar

¼ cup light corn syrup

¾ cup freshly squeezed lemon juice

1 cup whole milk

2 cups heavy cream

Pinch of kosher salt

INSTRUCTIONS:

1. Zest the lemons into a blender or food processor. Add the sugar and blend.
2. Add all the remaining ingredients and blend.
3. Chill for 2 hours, then pour into your ice cream maker and follow the manufacturer's directions.
4. Transfer to an airtight container and freeze for 4 hours or overnight.

Lemon Gingersnap

Here's an alternate base for lemon ice cream, with the addition of yummy gingersnap cookies.

INGREDIENTS:

⅓ cup granulated sugar
1 cup whole milk
2 cups heavy cream
1 (3.4 oz.) box instant lemon pudding mix (about ⅔ cup pudding powder)
¼ cup lemon juice
10–12 gingersnap cookies, broken into bite-sized pieces

INSTRUCTIONS:

1. Mix sugar with milk in a large bowl with a wire whisk. Stir until sugar is dissolved.
2. Add heavy cream, instant lemon pudding mix, and lemon juice. Stir with a wire whisk until fully blended.
3. Add to your ice cream maker and follow the manufacturer's directions.
4. While the ice cream is churning, break your cookies into pieces.
5. When the ice cream has reached soft-serve consistency, remove it from the ice cream maker and transfer it to an airtight container in layers, dropping cookie pieces on each layer.
6. Freeze for 4 hours or overnight.

Pie and Cheesecake

ICE CREAM FLAVORS

These flavors were my favorite to create! I wanted to get the ice cream to taste just like their namesake pies and cheesecakes. I've used several different types of ice cream bases. Some are a classic vanilla base, some use pudding mixes, and some use cream cheese and sour cream. Feel free to mix and match and create your own flavors!

Banana Cream Pie

Banana Cream Pie is my favorite kind of pie. (I used to eat it for breakfast! Does that mean I can eat this ice cream for breakfast?)

INGREDIENTS:

½ cup granulated sugar

1 cup whole milk

2 cups heavy cream

½ cup of instant banana cream pudding mix (the powder)

1–2 bananas cut in very small chunks

Your favorite pie crust, or my recipe for Pie Crust (pg. 138), baked and broken in pieces.

INSTRUCTIONS:

1. If making your own pie crust, prepare and bake. Set aside to cool while you make the ice cream.
2. Mix the whole milk and sugar together until the sugar has dissolved.
3. Add the instant banana cream pudding mix and begin stirring.
4. Add the 2 cups of heavy cream and continue stirring until everything is well-blended.
5. Pour into your ice cream maker and follow the manufacturer's directions.
6. A couple of minutes before turning off the machine, add your small banana pieces. Let the ice cream continue to churn until the bananas have been well distributed throughout the ice cream.
7. Transfer to an airtight container in layers, dropping the pie crust pieces on each layer. (You may only use about half of the pie crust).
8. Freeze for 4 hours or overnight.
9. Serve with a large dollop of Whipped Cream (pg. 135).

Lemon Meringue Pie

I kept this recipe a secret for a long time. I'd never had Lemon Meringue Pie Ice Cream (or even heard of it) and I wanted to be the only one who could make it! But not anymore—I want you to make it, too. It's utterly fantastic!

INGREDIENTS:

⅓ cup granulated sugar
1 cup whole milk
2 cups heavy cream
1 (3.4 oz.) box instant lemon pudding mix (about ⅔ cup of pudding powder)
¼ cup bottled or freshly squeezed lemon juice
Your favorite pie crust, or my recipe for Pie Crust (pg. 138), baked and broken in pieces.
Half of a (7 oz.) container of marshmallow crème

INSTRUCTIONS:

1. If making your own pie crust, prepare and bake. Set aside to cool while you make the ice cream.
2. Mix sugar with milk in a large bowl with a wire whisk. Stir 2 or 3 minutes until sugar is dissolved.
3. Add heavy cream, instant lemon pudding mix, and lemon juice. Stir with a wire whisk until fully blended.
4. Pour into your ice cream maker and follow the manufacturer's directions.
5. When ice cream has reached soft-serve consistency, transfer to an airtight container in layers, dropping some pie crust pieces and dollops of marshmallow crème on each layer.
6. Freeze for 4 hours or overnight.

Pumpkin Pie

Yep. It tastes just like pumpkin pie. Try it and you'll see!

INGREDIENTS:

¾ cup granulated sugar
¼ cup light corn syrup
1 cup whole milk
2 cups heavy cream
¾ cup pumpkin purée (not pumpkin pie filling)
1 ½ tsp. ground cinnamon
½ tsp. ground nutmeg
½ tsp. ground ginger
½ tsp. ground cloves
½ tsp. ground allspice
½ tsp. pure vanilla extract
⅛ tsp. salt
Your favorite pie crust, or my recipe for Pie Crust (pg. 138), baked and broken in pieces. You can also use vanilla sandwich cookies. (I typically use about half of a baked pie crust or 10 cookies)

INSTRUCTIONS:

1. If making your own pie crust, prepare and bake. Set aside to cool while you make the ice cream.
2. Warm the milk in the microwave for about 30 seconds in a microwave-safe medium-sized mixing bowl.
3. Add sugar to the warm milk and stir until the sugar is dissolved.
4. Add the rest of the ingredients (except the pie crust or cookies) and mix well.
5. Cover and put in refrigerator to chill for about 3 hours or overnight.
6. Pour into your ice cream maker and follow the manufacturer's directions. You'll want to churn this in 2 batches.
7. Transfer to an airtight container, gently folding in broken pie crust or cookie pieces.
8. Freeze for 4 hours or overnight.
9. When ready to serve, top with a dollop of Whipped Cream (pg. 135).

• FLAVOR VARIATION •

PUMPKIN CHOCOLATE SWIRL

1. Omit the pie crust, and drizzle melted chocolate, Chocolate Sauce (pg. 131) or Hot Fudge sauce (pg. 132) as you transfer your ice cream in layers to an airtight container for freezing.

Pumpkin Cheesecake

The graham cracker crust is what really takes this ice cream to the next level. Prepare to close your eyes in rapturous delight at the first bite! (Too dramatic? Well, try it and then let me know.)

INGREDIENTS:

One recipe for Graham Cracker Crust (pg. 136)
1 ¼ cups sugar
1 cup whole milk
2 cups heavy whipping cream
1 cup pumpkin purée (not pumpkin pie filling)
⅓ cup of instant vanilla pudding mix (the powder)
1 ½ tsp. ground cinnamon
½ tsp. ground nutmeg
½ tsp. ground ginger
½ tsp. ground cloves
½ tsp. ground allspice
⅛ tsp. salt
½ tsp. vanilla

INSTRUCTIONS:

1. In a large bowl, add the sugar to the milk and whisk until the sugar is dissolved.
2. Add the pumpkin and whisk with the milk and sugar.
3. Slowly add the heavy cream and instant vanilla pudding mix and whisk until everything is evenly distributed.
4. Add the pure vanilla extract and all the spices and mix well.
5. Cover and chill for 3 hours or overnight.
6. While the ice cream base is chilling, prepare the Cheesecake Crust and cool to room temperature. Then break into pieces.
7. When ready to churn, pour into your ice cream maker and follow the manufacturer's directions. You'll need to churn this in 2 batches.
8. Transfer to an airtight container in layers, dropping bite-sized broken pieces of the Graham Cracker Crust on each layer.
9. Freeze for 4 hours or overnight.

Lemon Raspberry Cheesecake

Lemon and raspberry are a wonderful flavor combination. If desired, you can substitute Fresh Lemon Ice Cream (pg. 63) for the ice cream base.

INGREDIENTS:

One recipe for Graham Cracker Crust (pg. 136)

One recipe for Berry Topping for Ice Cream (pg. 134, use only raspberries) or ½ cup raspberry jam

⅓ cup granulated sugar

1 cup whole milk

2 cups heavy cream

1 (3.4 oz.) box instant lemon pudding mix (about ⅔ cup of powder)

¼ cup bottled or freshly squeezed lemon juice

INSTRUCTIONS:

1. Make the Graham Cracker Crust and the Berry Topping (using raspberries) and set both aside at room temperature to cool for at least an hour.
2. When crust and topping have cooled, begin making the ice cream by mixing the sugar and milk together with a wire whisk. Stir until the sugar is dissolved.
3. Add heavy cream, instant lemon pudding, and lemon juice. Whisk until well mixed.
4. Add to your ice cream maker and follow the manufacturer's directions.
5. While ice cream is churning, break up the Graham Cracker Crust into bite-sized pieces.
6. When ice cream has reached soft-serve consistency, transfer to an airtight container, layering with the Graham Cracker Crust pieces and Berry Topping. (You will probably only use half of the Graham Cracker Crust and the Berry Topping). Save the remaining crust and topping to garnish individual portions of ice cream if desired.
7. Freeze for 4 hours or overnight.

Blueberry Cheesecake

This is Classic Vanilla Ice Cream with a ribbon of blueberry topping and delicious chunks of cheesecake crust. Alternatively, you can make a cream cheese/sour cream ice cream base by using the recipe for Strawberry Cheesecake Ice Cream on pg. 81.

INGREDIENTS:

One recipe for Graham Cracker Crust (pg. 136)

One recipe for Berry Topping for Ice Cream (pg. 134, using only blueberries)

¾ cup granulated sugar

1 cup whole milk

2 cups heavy cream

1 tsp. pure vanilla extract

INSTRUCTIONS:

1. Make the Graham Cracker Crust and the Berry Topping and set aside to cool at room temperature for at least an hour.
2. When crust and topping are cooled, begin making the ice cream by mixing the sugar and milk together with a wire whisk. Stir until the sugar is dissolved.
3. Add heavy cream and vanilla. Whisk until well mixed.
4. Add to your ice cream maker and follow the manufacturer's directions.
5. While ice cream is churning, break up the Graham Cracker Crust into bite-sized pieces.
6. When ice cream has reached soft-serve consistency, transfer to an airtight container, layering with the Graham Cracker Crust pieces and Berry Topping. (You will probably only use half of the crust and the berry topping.) Save the remaining crust and berry topping to garnish individual portions of ice cream if desired.
7. Freeze for 4 hours or overnight.

• FLAVOR VARIATION •

TRIPLE BERRY CHEESECAKE

1. Make Berry Topping for Ice Cream as it is written, with a mixture of raspberries, blueberries, and blackberries. Cool to room temperature and add to your ice cream in layers along with pieces of Graham Cracker Crust.

Strawberry Cheesecake

Cooked strawberries can often turn brown, which is why I suggest using strawberry jam here instead of making Berry Topping with strawberries.

INGREDIENTS:

One recipe of Graham Cracker Crust (pg. 136) or Chocolate Cookie Crust (pg. 137)

1 lemon, washed

8 ounces cream cheese

1 cup sour cream

¼ cup whole milk

¼ cup heavy cream

⅔ cup granulated sugar

½ cup strawberry jam

INSTRUCTIONS:

1. Make your Graham Cracker Crust or Chocolate Cookie Crust and set aside to cool.
2. Zest half of the lemon into a blender (you should have about ¾ teaspoon of lemon zest).
3. Add the cream cheese, sour cream, whole milk, heavy cream, and granulated sugar to the blender.
4. Blend on high speed for 45 seconds.
5. Chill the blended mixture for 1 hour.
6. When ready to churn, pour into your ice cream maker and follow the manufacturer's directions.
7. While the ice cream is churning, break your Graham Cracker Crust or Chocolate Cookie Crust into bite-sized pieces.
8. When ice cream has reached soft-serve consistency, transfer to an airtight container in layers, dropping pieces of the broken Graham Cracker Crust or Chocolate Cookie Crust, followed by a dollop of strawberry jam, on each layer (you may not use all the crust).
9. Freeze for 4 hours or overnight.

Lime Cheesecake

This ice cream has the perfect kick of lime. You'll love the tang created by the cream cheese and sour cream, too!

INGREDIENTS:

One recipe for Graham Cracker Crust (pg. 136)

1 lime, washed

½ cup bottled or freshly squeezed lime juice

8 ounces cream cheese

1 cup sour cream

¼ cup whole milk

¼ cup heavy cream

1 cup plus 2 Tbsp. granulated sugar

INSTRUCTIONS:

1. Prepare the Graham Cracker Crust and set aside to cool.
2. Zest the lime into a blender (you should end up with about 1 ½ teaspoons of lime zest).
3. Add the rest of the ingredients (minus the Graham Cracker Crust) to the blender and blend on high speed for 45 seconds.
4. Chill the blended mixture for 1 hour.
5. When ready to churn, pour into your ice cream maker and follow the manufacturer's directions.
6. While the ice cream is churning, break your Graham Cracker Crust into bite-sized pieces.
7. When ice cream has reached soft-serve consistency, transfer to an airtight container in layers, dropping pieces of the broken Graham Cracker Crust on each layer (you may not use all the crust).
8. Freeze for 4 hours or overnight.

Chocolate Cheesecake

This ice cream is super rich and packs a punch!
If you love Chocolate Cheesecake, this is a "must make!"

INGREDIENTS:

One recipe for Chocolate Cookie Crust (pg. 137)
8 ounces cream cheese
1 cup sour cream
¼ cup whole milk
¼ cup heavy cream
¾ cup granulated sugar
5 Tbsp. unsweetened cocoa powder

INSTRUCTIONS:

1. Make your Chocolate Cookie Crust and set aside to cool.
2. Add all the remaining ingredients to a blender and blend on high speed for 45 seconds.
3. Chill the blended mixture for 1 hour.
4. When ready to churn, pour into your ice cream maker and follow the manufacturer's directions.
5. While the ice cream is churning, break your Chocolate Cookie Crust into bite-sized pieces.
6. When ice cream has reached soft-serve consistency, transfer to an airtight container in layers, dropping pieces of the broken Chocolate Cookie Crust on each layer. (You may not use all the crust).
7. Freeze for 4 hours or overnight.
8. Note: You can add Chocolate Sauce (pg. 131) or room-temperature Hot Fudge Sauce (pg. 132) to this ice cream in layers as you transfer it to an airtight container after churning.

Fun and Creative

ICE CREAM FLAVORS

This section is for ice cream flavors that don't clearly fit into any other category, but still had to be in the book! Don't worry—even though some of the flavors might be unexpected, you'll still be able to easily find the ingredients, and everything will be delicious!

S'mores

Ah, those wonderful summer nights sitting around the campfire, roasting marshmallows and eating s'mores. For those great campfire flavors any time of year, make this S'mores Ice Cream!

INGREDIENTS:

⅔ cup granulated sugar
1 cup whole milk
2 cups heavy cream
1 tsp. pure vanilla extract
3 graham cracker sheets, broken into bite-sized pieces
½ cup marshmallow crème
¼ cup semi-sweet chocolate chips
¾ tsp. coconut oil

INSTRUCTIONS:

1. In a large bowl, mix the sugar and milk together until sugar is dissolved.
2. Add the heavy cream and pure vanilla extract and mix well.
3. Pour into your ice cream maker and follow the manufacturer's directions.
4. While the ice cream is churning, melt the chocolate chips along with the coconut oil in a small pan over low heat on the stove, stirring constantly. After melted, set aside to cool slightly.
5. When ice cream is done churning, transfer to an airtight container, layering with the graham cracker pieces and marshmallow crème, and drizzling each layer with the melted chocolate.
6. Freeze for 4 hours or overnight.

Peppermint White Chocolate

This ice cream was inspired by my favorite Christmas cookies containing candy canes and white chocolate. If desired, you can add a drop or two of red food coloring to make the ice cream a more vibrant pink.

INGREDIENTS:

¾ cup sugar

1 cup whole milk

2 cups heavy cream

½ tsp. pure vanilla extract

10–15 drops dōTERRA® peppermint essential oil, or 1 tsp. peppermint extract, to taste

½ cup white chocolate chips plus ¼ tsp. vegetable oil

¾ cup crushed candy canes

INSTRUCTIONS:

1. Mix milk and sugar together until sugar is dissolved.
2. Add heavy cream, vanilla extract, and peppermint oil or extract, and mix well.
3. Pour into your ice cream maker and follow the manufacturer's directions.
4. While ice cream is churning, crush candy canes. (I put mine in a blender and pulse until finely chopped.) Set aside.
5. Put white chocolate chips and vegetable oil in a small saucepan on the stove. Heat over medium-low heat, stirring constantly, until fully melted and smooth. Remove from heat.
6. About 5 minutes before ice cream is done churning, add the crushed candy canes.
7. When ice cream reaches soft-serve consistency, transfer to an airtight container in layers, drizzling the melted white chocolate on each layer.
8. Freeze for 4 hours or overnight.

Sweet Potato with Pecan Streusel

Who doesn't love the sweet potato casserole at Thanksgiving? Even if you're saying, "Not me!" give this ice cream a try. You just might become a fan!

INGREDIENTS:

One recipe for Pecan Streusel Topping (pg. 141)

1 small sweet potato or yam (about ½ pound)

¾ cup brown sugar, lightly packed

¼ cup light corn syrup

1 cup whole milk

2 cups heavy cream

1 tsp. cinnamon

¼ cup marshmallow crème

INSTRUCTIONS:

1. Heat your oven to 350°F.
2. Wash your sweet potato or yam and prick in several places with a fork. Wrap in aluminum foil and bake for 1 to 1 ½ hours, until very tender when pierced with a fork.
3. Remove from the oven, unwrap, and cool until able to be handled—at least 30 minutes. While your sweet potato is cooling, prepare your Pecan Streusel Topping. Cool for at least 1 hour.
4. Once your Pecan Streusel Topping is out of the oven, your sweet potato should be cool enough to handle. Peel the skin off the baked sweet potato (you should be able to easily remove it with your fingers).
5. Put the sweet potato into a blender and blend on high speed until a very smooth purée is formed. Separate out ¾ cup of purée and refrigerate for at least 1 hour. (If you have extra purée, save it for another use.)
6. Once the sweet potato purée has chilled, begin making the rest of your ice cream base.
7. In a large mixing bowl, add your brown sugar, light corn syrup, and milk. Whisk well until the sugar is dissolved.
8. Add the pumpkin purée and cinnamon and mix well.
9. Add the heavy cream and mix well.
10. Pour into your ice cream maker and follow the manufacturer's directions. I recommend churning this recipe in two batches.
11. While the ice cream is churning, break your Pecan Streusel Topping into bite-sized pieces.
12. When ice cream has reached soft-serve consistency, transfer it to an airtight container in layers, dropping pieces of Pecan Streusel Topping and dollops of marshmallow crème on each layer. (You will not use all the Pecan Streusel Topping.) Freeze for 4 hours or overnight.

1 tsp
1/2 tsp
1 tbsp
1/4 tsp

Vanilla Spice

This recipe uses my favorite herbal tea and its wonderful spices, including cinnamon, cardamom, ginger, cloves, nutmeg, and black pepper.

INGREDIENTS:

4 tea bags of your favorite chai or spicy herbal tea (my favorite is Bengal Spice by Celestial Seasonings)
⅔ cup granulated sugar
1 cup whole milk
2 cups heavy cream
1 tsp. pure vanilla extract
2 tsp. ground cinnamon
1 tsp. ground cardamom
½ tsp. ground ginger
½ tsp. ground cloves
½ tsp. ground nutmeg
Pinch of black pepper

INSTRUCTIONS:

1. Heat 1 cup of milk in a small saucepan on the stove over medium-high heat until steaming.
2. Remove the milk from the heat and add all the tea bags to the hot milk. Allow to steep for 30 minutes.
3. Remove the tea bags, pressing them against the side of the pan to get as much flavor out of them as you can. Discard the tea bags.
4. Chill the tea-infused milk for 2 hours or until cold.
5. When ready to make the ice cream, add the tea-infused milk to a large bowl, along with the remaining ingredients. Stir well.
6. Pour into your ice cream maker and follow the manufacturer's directions.
7. Transfer to an airtight container and freeze for 4 hours or overnight.

Maple Walnut

Maple Walnut is my mom's favorite flavor of ice cream. I had to include it here for her, and for you, too, because it's incredibly delicious!

INGREDIENTS:

One recipe Candied Walnuts (pg. 124), or ¾ cup chopped walnuts (if you don't want to use candied walnuts)

¾ cup pure maple syrup (Grade A amber or dark amber) not pancake syrup or sugar free syrup

1 Tbsp. granulated sugar

1 cup whole milk

2 cups heavy cream

½ tsp. maple extract

INSTRUCTIONS:

1. If using candied walnuts, prepare them first and set aside to cool.
2. Pour the maple syrup into a small saucepan. Heat over medium-high for about 30 minutes, stirring occasionally, until syrup has been reduced to a little more than half a cup. Add the granulated sugar and stir.
3. Pour into a heat-safe container and refrigerate for at least 2 hours, until cold.
4. In a large bowl, mix together the milk and cream. Add the chilled, reduced maple syrup and maple extract. Mix well.
5. Pour into your ice cream maker and follow the manufacturer's directions.
6. Add the chopped walnuts during the last minute of churning. If using candied walnuts, do not add them to the ice cream while it is still churning. Instead, drop them on your ice cream in layers as you transfer the ice cream to an airtight container.
7. Freeze for 4 hours or overnight.

Root Beer

When I was a kid, this was my favorite flavor of ice cream.
Now that I'm adult, I've never seen it in the store, but luckily, I can make my own!

INGREDIENTS:

¾ cup granulated sugar

1 cup whole milk

2 cups heavy cream

2 Tbsp. root beer extract

1 tsp. pure vanilla extract

INSTRUCTIONS:

1. In a large mixing bowl, whisk the granulated sugar and milk together until the sugar is dissolved.
2. Add the remaining ingredients and mix well.
3. Pour into your ice cream maker and follow the manufacturer's directions.
4. When ice cream has reached soft-serve consistency, transfer to an airtight container and freeze for 4 hours or overnight.

Fruit Sorbets

ICE CREAM FLAVORS

One of my daughters is allergic to dairy, so sorbets are her jam. We love sorbet at our house, and I bet you love it at your house, too. It's a wonderful way to use fresh or frozen fruit, and so quick and easy to make.

If you find that your sorbet is too hard to scoop after freezing, you can wait for it to thaw a little, or scrape the surface with a fork to create an Italian granita.

Strawberry

Wonderfully bright and fresh, this is the quintessential summer treat.

INGREDIENTS:

1 cup granulated sugar

1 cup water

1 quart fresh strawberries, washed and stemmed (about 4 cups)

4 Tbsp. fresh lemon or lime juice

¼ cup light corn syrup

INSTRUCTIONS:

1. Add the water and sugar to a small saucepan on the stove. Bring to a boil, then reduce the heat and simmer the mixture without stirring until the sugar has completely dissolved.
2. Remove from the heat and cool completely.
3. Add the strawberries and lemon or lime juice to a blender or food processor. Pulse 8–10 times to chop up the strawberries. Then blend on high speed until the strawberries are completely puréed, with no lumps.
4. If desired, strain the strawberry purée through a fine mesh strainer to remove any seeds.
5. Mix the strawberry purée, cooled sugar water, and light corn syrup. Refrigerate for at least 1 hour.
6. Pour into your ice cream maker and follow the manufacturer's directions.
7. When the sorbet has reached soft-serve consistency, remove from the ice cream maker and transfer to an airtight container.
8. Freeze for 4 hours or overnight.

Peach

Growing up, we had a peach tree in our yard. We always had more peaches than we knew what to do with. If you find yourself in a similar situation, here's your solution!

INGREDIENTS:

10 ripe peaches, peeled and sliced

⅔ cup granulated sugar

½ cup light corn syrup

2 Tbsp. fresh lime or lemon juice

INSTRUCTIONS:

1. Add all the ingredients to a blender or food processor. Pulse to chop up the peaches. Then blend until everything is smooth.
2. Cover and refrigerate for at least 1 hour.
3. Add to your ice cream maker and follow the manufacturer's directions.
4. When the sorbet has reached soft-serve consistency, remove from the ice cream maker and transfer to an airtight container.
5. Freeze for 4 hours or overnight.

Lemon

For all you lemon lovers out there, you can't get a more pure, fresh lemon taste than this Lemon Sorbet!

INGREDIENTS:

2 ½ cups water, divided

1¼ cup granulated sugar

¼ cup light corn syrup

6 lemons, washed and chilled

INSTRUCTIONS:

1. Put ½ cup of the water and the granulated sugar into a small saucepan.
2. Zest 2 of the lemons directly into the saucepan with the sugar.
3. Heat over high heat until boiling, stirring occasionally until all the sugar has dissolved.
4. Remove from the heat and add the light corn syrup. Gently stir until the corn syrup is incorporated.
5. Add the remaining 2 cups of water and then refrigerate for at least 2 hours.
6. Juice your chilled lemons to get about 1 cup of fresh lemon juice. If desired, strain the pulp.
7. Add the fresh lemon juice to the chilled sugar water. Mix.
8. Add to your ice cream maker and churn according to the manufacturer's directions.
9. If desired, add 1 or 2 drops of yellow food coloring while churning.
10. When the sorbet has reached soft-serve consistency, remove from the ice cream maker and transfer to an airtight container.
11. Freeze for 4 hours or overnight.

Lime

If desired, add a drop of green food coloring to give this Lime Sorbet a traditional green color.

INGREDIENTS:

2 ¼ cups water, divided

1¼ cup granulated sugar

1 lime, washed

¼ cup light corn syrup

¾ cup lime juice (from about 9 limes, or you can use bottled lime juice), chilled

INSTRUCTIONS:

1. Mix 1 cup of water with the sugar in a saucepan. Zest the lime into the saucepan and heat until the sugar is dissolved.
2. Add the light corn syrup and remaining water. Chill for at least 2 hours.
3. Just before churning, add the lime juice.
4. Add to your ice cream maker and churn according to the manufacturer's directions.
5. If desired, add 1 or 2 drops of green food coloring while churning.
6. When the sorbet has reached soft-serve consistency, remove from the ice cream maker and transfer to an airtight container.
7. Freeze for 4 hours or overnight.

Watermelon

One day, we bought an ENORMOUS watermelon in Green River, Utah (my dad's hometown, and the Watermelon Mecca of the Universe, according to him). We couldn't eat all of it, so I made this tasty watermelon sorbet!

INGREDIENTS:

6 cups fresh watermelon chunks, de-seeded

½ cup granulated sugar

pinch of kosher salt

1 Tbsp. lime juice

INSTRUCTIONS:

1. Purée the watermelon chunks in a blender. You want 3 cups of purée. (Measure just the juice—not the foam).
2. Pour ½ cup of the purée into a small saucepan. Add the sugar and pinch of kosher salt.
3. Place pan on the stove over low heat. Stir occasionally until the sugar has dissolved. Remove from the heat. (This does not need to get very hot).
4. Pour the sugar/salt/watermelon purée mixture back into the rest of the watermelon purée. Refrigerate for at least 1 hour.
5. When ready to churn, add to your ice cream maker and follow the manufacturer's instructions. (If the mixture stops moving through the machine, use a small spoon or spatula inserted through the hole in the lid of your ice cream maker to help push the mixture through the dasher and keep it moving.)
6. When soft-serve consistency and no longer watery, transfer to an airtight container and freeze for 4 hours or overnight.
7. Alternately, you can eat this right away, but it will have a more slushy consistency.

Piña Colada

If you've ever had a Dole Whip® and loved it, your wildest dreams are about to come true! My recipe is dairy-free (made with coconut milk), so it's great for people with milk allergies.

INGREDIENTS:

1 cup granulated sugar

2 ¼ cup pineapple juice

1 can unsweetened coconut milk (about 13.5 fluid ounces)

INSTRUCTIONS:

1. Add all ingredients to a blender and blend until smooth.
2. Refrigerate for 2 hours.
3. When ready to churn, pour into your ice cream maker and follow the manufacturer's directions.
4. Transfer to an airtight container and freeze for 4 hours or overnight.
5. For the classic Dole Whip® texture, eat immediately after churning.

Mango

I highly suggest using frozen mango chunks for this recipe. But if you don't mind peeling mangoes and cutting off the flesh, feel free to use fresh mangoes instead.

INGREDIENTS:

4 cups fresh or frozen mango chunks

⅔ cup granulated sugar

2 Tbsp. corn syrup

⅔ cup water or coconut milk

1 Tbsp. lime juice

INSTRUCTIONS:

1. If using frozen mango chunks, allow them to thaw slightly in the refrigerator for about 4 hours prior to churning your sorbet.
2. When ready to churn, place all the ingredients into a blender and purée.
3. Pour into your ice cream maker and follow the manufacturer's directions.
4. Transfer to an airtight container and freeze for 4 hours or overnight.

Add-ins and Toppings

ICE CREAM FLAVORS

Here's where things get really fun! You can come up with infinite ice cream variations, just by changing what you throw in. Mix and match these add-ins to create your own amazing flavor combos!

Decadent Chocolate Brownies

This makes a whole 9x13-inch pan of brownies. They are hands down, my favorite brownies ever. There will be plenty for you to eat and still have leftovers to add to your ice cream.

INGREDIENTS:

- 3 cups semi-sweet chocolate chips
- 1 cup butter, salted or unsalted (two sticks)
- 5 large eggs
- 2 cups granulated sugar
- 1 Tbsp. pure vanilla extract
- 1 ½ cups flour
- 1 tsp. baking powder
- ¼ tsp. salt
- 1 cup walnuts or pecans, coarsely chopped (optional)

INSTRUCTIONS:

1. Preheat oven to 350°F.
2. Melt the chocolate chips and butter together over low heat on the stove, stirring frequently. Alternately, you can heat the butter and chocolate chips in the microwave in 30-second increments, stirring after each time until smooth. When completely melted and incorporated, set aside to cool slightly.
3. In a separate bowl, mix together the eggs and sugar.
4. Add the vanilla and the melted chocolate mixture and stir.
5. Add the flour, baking powder, and salt. Mix well. Add nuts if desired.
6. Pour into a greased 9x13 pan and bake for 35-45 minutes, or until a toothpick comes out of the middle with just a few crumbs.
7. Remove from the oven and let cool before cutting.

Chocolate Chip Cookie Dough

This egg-free edible cookie dough makes just a small amount, perfect for one batch of ice cream.

INGREDIENTS:

2 Tbsp. salted butter, melted
¼ cup packed brown sugar
⅛ tsp. salt
⅛ tsp. pure vanilla extract
1 Tbsp. milk
6 Tbsp. all-purpose flour
2 Tbsp. mini chocolate chips

INSTRUCTIONS:

1. Prepare your cookie dough by mixing together the melted butter and packed brown sugar.
2. Add the salt, vanilla, and milk and stir together.
3. Add the flour and mix until incorporated.
4. Add 2 tablespoons of mini chocolate chips and stir until well-distributed.
5. Use a ½ teaspoon measuring spoon to portion the dough into small balls about the size of marbles. Roll between the palms of your hands to make smooth, if desired.
6. Cover and chill until ready to use.

Peanut Butter Cookie Dough

The key to making a smooth edible peanut butter cookie dough is to use powdered sugar instead of granulated sugar.

INGREDIENTS:

2 Tbsp. salted butter, softened

2 Tbsp. peanut butter

¼ cup powdered sugar

dash of pure vanilla extract

dash of salt

1 Tbsp. milk

6 Tbsp. all-purpose flour

INSTRUCTIONS:

1. Mix the softened butter and peanut butter together in a small bowl.
2. Add the powdered sugar and slowly mix until the sugar disappears.
3. Add the pure vanilla extract, salt, and milk and mix well.
4. Add the flour and mix just until the flour disappears. Dough should be soft, but hold its shape. Add more flour if necessary to get the desired consistency.
5. Use a ½ teaspoon measuring spoon to portion the dough into small balls about the size of marbles. Roll between the palms of your hands to make smooth, if desired.
6. Cover and chill until ready to use.

Candied Walnuts

Here are three ways to sweeten up the walnuts you add to your ice cream. You can use any of these methods with any type of nut, or with pepitas (green pumpkin seeds). You can also experiment with adding spices, such as cinnamon, cloves, and nutmeg before heating your sugar.

INGREDIENTS:

¼ cup granulated sugar

¼ tsp. salt

¾ cup chopped walnuts

INSTRUCTIONS:

1. Lay a piece of parchment paper on your countertop.
2. Add the granulated sugar to a small skillet and heat over medium heat, stirring occasionally with a wooden spoon or rubber scraper.
3. After a few minutes, the sugar will begin to melt and form clumps. Keep stirring the sugar until it completely melts and is a light golden color.
4. Add the salt and stir.
5. Keep stirring the sugar until it turns a medium-dark amber color. You must stir this constantly and watch the color carefully. If it gets too dark, it means your sugar has burned and it will be very bitter. Better to under-cook than over-cook.
6. Remove from the heat and immediately stir in the chopped walnuts. Stir quickly to cover the walnuts in the melted sugar, and then pour out onto your parchment paper.
7. Use two forks to quickly separate your candied walnuts. The sugar syrup will harden quickly.
8. Cool completely. Break up or cut into smaller pieces if desired.

• FLAVOR VARIATIONS •

CARAMEL WALNUTS

1. Add 2 tablespoons of brown sugar and 1 teaspoon of water to a small frying pan. Heat on medium heat.
2. When the sugar has dissolved into the water and become bubbly, add ½ cup of whole walnuts and stir to coat.
3. Keep stirring until most of the moisture has evaporated.
4. Pour the walnuts out onto parchment paper or waxed paper lightly sprayed with cooking spray. Cool completely. These will not harden, but will have a soft, caramel exterior.

SUGARED WALNUTS

1. Add 2 tablespoons of granulated sugar to a small frying pan.
2. Add ½ cup chopped walnuts and stir with the sugar on medium heat. The sugar will start to melt and stick to the walnuts.
3. When the sugar has all melted and is stuck to the walnuts, turn the nuts out onto parchment paper or waxed paper lightly sprayed with cooking spray. Cool completely.

Caramel Sauce

This caramel sauce stays soft in ice cream, even when frozen. Add it before freezing, pour it over the top when serving, or just eat it by the spoonful. You can cut down on the salt if you want less of a salted caramel flavor.

INGREDIENTS:

¾ cup granulated sugar

½ cup plus 2 Tbsp. heavy cream

¼ cup salted butter (half a stick)

½ tsp. kosher salt

INSTRUCTIONS:

1. In a medium-sized saucepan, cook the sugar over medium-high heat until melted and medium-dark amber. (Sugar will clump up first, then turn a light golden color, then get darker until it's a lovely deep amber color.)
2. Once sugar has reached the desired color, carefully pour the heavy cream down the side of the pan, stirring constantly until smooth. (I highly recommend that you wear oven mitts while adding the cream and stirring. The cream creates a lot of steam, and it is easy to burn your hands.)
3. Keep stirring until any clumps are gone. If necessary, use a wire whisk.
4. Remove from the heat and add the kosher salt. Stir.
5. Let cool to room temperature. Caramel will thicken as it cools.
6. Cover and store in the refrigerator. Bring to room temperature before serving, or heat for 15 seconds in the microwave.

Dulce de Leche (two ways)

Dulce de Leche is a great substitute for caramel in ice cream recipes. It tastes very similar to caramel and does not freeze, so it stays soft in your ice cream.

INGREDIENTS:

1 (14 oz.) can sweetened condensed milk

INSTRUCTIONS METHOD 1:

1. Fill a large stock pot with water. Place the can of sweetened condensed milk at the bottom of the pan and place on the stove over high heat.
2. Boil the water for 3 hours (you may need to add more water if too much evaporates). Make sure the can is always completely covered with water.
3. Carefully remove the can with tongs and cool to room temperature.

INSTRUCTIONS METHOD 2:

1. Heat your oven to 425°F.
2. Open the can of sweetened condensed milk and pour it into an 8x8 or 9x9 glass baking dish. Cover with foil and set inside of a larger baking dish (like a roasting pan).
3. Place the large baking dish with the smaller baking dish into the oven.
4. Pour hot water into the larger baking dish until it comes half-way up the side of the smaller baking dish.
5. Bake for 1 to 1 ½ hours. Add more water during baking if necessary. (Be careful when opening the oven not to lean in too quickly and get burned by steam.)
6. Check the color of the sweetened condensed milk. When it is a dark butterscotch color, it is done.
7. Remove from the oven and cool to room temperature.

Hot Pepper Honey

In Italy, all the restaurants have vessels of olive oil with hot pepper flakes in them. I figured I'd try the same trick for honey, and the results are magical!

INGREDIENTS:

½ cup honey
1 tsp. red pepper flakes

INSTRUCTIONS:

1. Mix together in a glass jar.
2. Store at room temperature.

Chocolate Sauce

Drizzle this over the top of your ice cream or add it before freezing to make ribbons of chocolate.

INGREDIENTS:

½ cup granulated sugar

⅓ cup light corn syrup

½ cup water

6 Tbsp. unsweetened cocoa powder

1 tsp. pure vanilla extract

INSTRUCTIONS:

1. Add all the ingredients except the vanilla to a small saucepan.
2. Cook over medium heat, stirring occasionally.
3. When the mixture begins to boil, cook for 1 more minute, stirring constantly.
4. Remove from heat and add the vanilla.
5. Let cool to room temperature.
6. Cover and store in the refrigerator.

Hot Fudge Sauce

You can drizzle this warm over ice cream or chill it in the refrigerator. It will harden into a ganache when chilled or frozen, but will still be soft and pliable. It's the perfect "fudge" to layer in your ice cream!

INGREDIENTS:

¼ cup plus 2 Tbsp. heavy cream

2 Tbsp. brown sugar

2 Tbsp. unsweetened cocoa powder

¼ cup light corn syrup

3 ounces dark or semi-sweet chocolate chips (about ½ cup)

2 tsp. salted butter

¼ tsp. pure vanilla extract

INSTRUCTIONS:

1. Add the cream, brown sugar, cocoa powder, and light corn syrup to a small saucepan. Bring to a boil and stir for 30 seconds while boiling.
2. Remove from heat and add the chocolate chips and butter. Stir until the chocolate chips are melted and everything is smooth.
3. Add the vanilla and stir. Serve warm, or chill and allow to firm up.

Chocolate Shell

This stays liquid at room temperature, but freezes on contact with ice cream and turns into a crispy shell.

INGREDIENTS:

1 cup semi-sweet or dark chocolate chips

½ cup coconut oil

Pinch of salt

INSTRUCTIONS:

1. Add all the ingredients to a microwave-safe bowl and heat in the microwave for 1 minute.
2. Remove and stir with a rubber scraper. If needed, return to the microwave in 30-second increments, stirring after each time.
3. When the chocolate chips have almost melted, just keep stirring the mixture until they completely melt and the mixture is smooth.
4. Drizzle on top of ice cream and watch the magic happen!
5. Store at room temperature. If it hardens, warm it up in the microwave in 15-second increments until it liquefies.

Berry Topping

It's best to mix and match most types of berries in this recipe. If using strawberries, be aware that the berries may turn brown during cooking.

INGREDIENTS:

¼ cup granulated sugar

1 ½ tsp. cornstarch

¼ cup water

⅔ cup blueberries, blackberries, or raspberries (or a combination of all three), fresh or frozen

1 ½ tsp. lemon juice

INSTRUCTIONS:

1. Combine sugar and corn starch in a pan on the stove. Add the water gradually, whisking until smooth over medium heat.
2. Add berries and lemon juice.
3. Bring to a boil, then reduce heat to low.
4. Simmer, uncovered, until slightly thickened.
5. Slightly mash the berries with a potato masher, or cool to room temperature and pour the whole mixture into a blender and purée. Strain if desired.
6. Chill before adding to ice cream, or add warm with Crumble Topping (pg. 140) when serving.

Whipped Cream

Do you have a little heavy cream left over, but not enough to make a batch of ice cream? This is the perfect solution!

INGREDIENTS:

1 cup heavy whipping cream

3 Tbsp. granulated sugar

1 tsp. pure vanilla extract

INSTRUCTIONS:

1. Add all the ingredients to a large mixing bowl. Whip with beaters or whisk attachment (if using a stand mixer) on high speed for 2-3 minutes until stiff peaks form.
2. Chill until ready to serve.

Graham Cracker Crust

Get ready—your kitchen will never smell more heavenly than when this Graham Cracker Crust is baking in the oven!

INGREDIENTS:

1 cup graham cracker crumbs (about 8 sheets of graham crackers, pulverized in a food processor or blender)

1 Tbsp. granulated sugar

¼ tsp. cinnamon

5 Tbsp. salted butter, melted

INSTRUCTIONS:

1. Heat your oven to 350°F.
2. Add all the ingredients together in a medium-sized mixing bowl.
3. Gently stir together until the graham cracker crumbs are evenly coated with butter.
4. Press into the bottom of an 8x8 or 9x9 baking dish, cake pan, or pie plate.
5. Bake for 10–15 minutes, until the edges are just beginning to brown.
6. Cool completely at room temperature.

Chocolate Cookie Crust

*Don't be tempted to remove the filling from the cookies.
The crust just isn't as good without it.*

INGREDIENTS:

12 Oreos®, or other chocolate sandwich cookies
4 Tbsp. salted butter, melted

INSTRUCTIONS:

1. Heat your oven to 350°F.
2. Add the Oreos®, or chocolate sandwich cookies to a food processor or blender. Do not remove the filling from the cookies.
3. Pulse, and then blend until you get fine crumbs. You'll want about 1 cup of crumbs. Add more cookies if necessary to get the desired amount of crumbs.
4. Pour the melted butter into the blender or food processor and pulse until the butter is evenly distributed throughout.
5. Pour the crumbs into an 8x8 or 9x9 baking dish, cake pan, or pie plate.
6. Bake for 10 minutes.
7. Cool completely at room temperature.

Pie Crust

This recipe makes enough for a single pie crust. No need to worry about chilled ingredients or rolling anything out. Just press into a pie plate and bake!

INGREDIENTS:

1 cup all-purpose flour
¼ tsp. salt
1 tsp. granulated sugar
¼ cup vegetable oil
1 ½ Tbsp. water

INSTRUCTIONS:

1. Heat your oven to 400°F.
2. Add all the ingredients together in a medium-sized bowl.
3. Mix with a fork. Use your hands if necessary to get all the ingredients to come together.
4. Press into the bottom and up the sides of a pie plate. Prick with a fork. (No need to make this neat or roll it out. It's just going to be broken up and added to ice cream.)
5. Bake for 10–11 minutes, until barely starting to brown. Cool completely at room temperature.

Pretzel Topping

This sweet and salty crust is a great addition to almost any flavor of ice cream.

INGREDIENTS:

6 Tbsp. salted butter, softened

1 ½ Tbsp. granulated sugar

2 cups pretzels

INSTRUCTIONS:

1. Heat your oven to 350°F.
2. Add your pretzels to a blender or food processor and pulse until chopped into small pieces. Do not pulverize into crumbs.
3. Add the softened butter and sugar to the blender and pulse a few more times to evenly distribute the butter throughout the pretzels.
4. Press mixture into the bottom of an 8x8 or 9x9 baking dish, cake pan, or pie plate.
5. Bake for 10 minutes.
6. Cool completely at room temperature.

Crumble Topping

After baking and cooling, break this up and drop it by hand into your ice cream when transferring it to an airtight container for freezing. Don't add it while churning or it will break apart and make your ice cream gritty.

INGREDIENTS:

¼ cup granulated sugar

¼ cup packed brown sugar

¼ cup all-purpose flour

¼ cup oats (not instant)

¼–½ tsp. ground cinnamon, to taste

5 Tbsp. cold, salted butter

INSTRUCTIONS:

1. Heat your oven to 350°F.
2. Cut butter into small chunks.
3. Put all ingredients (including butter) into a bowl and cut with a pastry cutter or two knives until ingredients are mixed and crumbly. (Alternately, you can put all the ingredients into a food processor and pulse just until the butter is evenly distributed and the mixture is still crumbly. Be sure not to over mix!)
4. Press into an 8x8 or 9x9 baking dish, cake pan, or pie plate and bake for 20 minutes or until golden brown. Cool completely at room temperature.

Pecan Streusel

Feel free to leave the coconut out of this recipe if you're not a coconut lover.

INGREDIENTS:

2 Tbsp. salted butter
½ cup packed brown sugar
2 Tbsp. plus 1 tsp. all-purpose flour
½ tsp. ground cinnamon
½ cup chopped pecans
¼ cup shredded coconut, sweetened or unsweetened

INSTRUCTIONS:

1. Heat your oven to 350°F.
2. Melt the butter in a microwave-safe bowl, or in a small saucepan on the stove over low heat.
3. Add the brown sugar to the melted butter and stir.
4. Add the cinnamon and flour and stir. Mixture will look like a paste.
5. Add the chopped pecans and shredded coconut. Stir.
6. Pour the mixture into an 8x8 or 9x9 baking dish, cake pan, or pie plate. Press down gently. Bake for 20 minutes.
7. Cool completely at room temperature.

FINAL WORDS

I hope you've had as much fun making and eating ice cream as I had writing this book!

Undoubtedly, you've discovered new flavors of ice cream that have become family favorites. Now I encourage you to experiment and make up your own flavors.

Be sure to revisit the section on ice cream chemistry to increase the odds that you'll be happy with your experiments. I often make half-batches of ice cream while I'm tinkering with flavors so that I don't end up with a lot of ice cream I don't like. Whatever you decide to do, you'd better make more room in your freezer! You're going to need it!

ACKNOWLEDGMENTS

Although this book was a dream of mine from the very start, it would never have come to fruition without the help of my family, my team at Cedar Fort, and a few miracles from above.

Thanks to my girls, Julianna, Natalie, and Kate. From being taste-testers, to suggesting flavors, to helping with food styling, this book really shines because of you. Your creativity and fresh perspectives saved the day many times, especially when I had run out of new ways to photograph ice cream.

Huge thanks to my husband Jacob who has never once questioned my entrepreneurial ideas, but has been unendingly supportive of them all, even when I had no idea what I was doing. Your business experience and calm head gave me the assurance that I could do whatever I wanted to do. You are the best business partner and life partner a girl could ever have.

Becky Clayton, I offer my sincere gratitude for the time and expertise you put into proofreading and editing this book to get it ready for submission. You're such a great cheerleader, and I'm so blessed to have you as my friend.

To the readers of my blog, Beautiful Life and Home, you are not random people across the world—you are my friends. Thank you for your encouragement and support.

And to the team at Cedar Fort, especially Dru Huffaker and Shawnda Craig, you've made my dream a reality. I literally couldn't have done it without you!

Finally, I owe everything to my Heavenly Father, who always seems to have perfectly-timed surprises up His sleeve.

Thank you.

Love,

Melissa

METRIC CONVERSION CHART

Volume		Weight		Temperature	
U.S.	Metric	U.S.	Metric	°F	°C
1 tsp.	5 mL	½ oz.	15 g	250	120
1 Tbsp.	15 mL	1 oz.	30 g	300	150
¼ cup	60 mL	3 oz.	90 g	325	160
⅓ cup	80 mL	4 oz.	115 g	350	180
½ cup	125 mL	8 oz.	225 g	375	190
⅔ cup	160 mL	12 oz.	350 g	400	200
¾ cup	180 mL	1 lb.	450 g	425	220
1 cup	250 mL	2¼ lb.	1 kg	450	230

∽ ICE CREAM AND SORBET INDEX ∾

ADD-INS AND TOPPINGS INDEX

ABOUT THE AUTHOR

MELISSA B. HOWELL used to be a pretty bad cook. In fact, she once thought it would be a good idea to cut up 10 pounds of onions all at once—It was not a good idea. Luckily, she learned from her mistakes, and now people think her cooking is quite fantastic. In addition to developing ice cream recipes, she is also a professional photographer and has created her own online personality-based home organizing program. When she is not watching Asian dramas, you can find her in the kitchen whipping up something new and delicious (and making a huge mess!). Melissa has one handsome husband and three beautiful daughters and lives in Denver, Colorado. Explore more at her website, beautifullifeandhome.com.